The Awakening of the Soul

Muhammad ibn 'Abd al-Malik Ibn Tufayl

Alpha Editions

This edition published in 2022

ISBN: 9789356159402

Design and Setting By

Alpha Editions
www.alphaedis.com

Email - info@alphaedis.com

Table of Contents

EDITORIAL NOTE

The object of the Editors of this series is a very definite one. They desire above all things that, in their humble way, these books shall be the ambassadors of good-will and understanding between East and West—the old world of Thought and the new of Action. In this endeavour, and in their own sphere, they are but followers of the highest example in the land. They are confident that a deeper knowledge of the great ideals and lofty philosophy of Oriental thought may help to a revival of that true spirit of Charity which neither despises nor fears the nations of another creed and colour.

L. CRANMER-BYNG.
S. A. KAPADIA.

THE NORTHBROOK SOCIETY,
21, Cromwell Road,
Kensington, S.W.

INTRODUCTION

It is to two English scholars, father and son, Edward Pococke, senior and junior, that the world is indebted for the knowledge of one of the most charming productions Arabian philosophy can boast of.

Generally looked upon as a subject of repulsive aridity, in its strange combination of the most heterogeneous philosophical systems, devoid of the grace and charm of attractive style, unbrightened by brilliancy of wit or spirit, Arabian philosophy has, for centuries past, been subject to sad and undeserved neglect.

Yet I cannot imagine a better and more eloquent refutation of this erroneous view than a rendering, in fresh garb, of this romance of Hayy Ibn Yokdhan, simple and ingenuous, yet fragrant with poetry and withal fraught with deep philosophical problems the interest in which I wish to revive.

It was in the year 1671 that there was published by the Oxford University Press, as one of its first issues of Arabic texts, a book called, "Philosophus autodidactus," edited by Edward Pococke the son, together with a Latin translation. It had a preface that bore the signature of Edward Pococke, the father, and this fact alone was sufficient to stamp it at once as a work in which vast erudition and thoroughness of investigation had joined hands—for both these *savants* were men of wide reputation and brilliant attainments.

England, that has put students of Oriental lore under such large obligations, has never given to the world a greater Arabic scholar than Edward Pococke, "the Glory and Ornament of his Age and Nation," the famous author of the "Specimen historiæ Arabum"; a veritable store-house of historical, scientific, literary, and religious information, and the equally famous editor of the annals of Eutychius and of the history of Dynasties by Abul faradj.

In the splendid array of famous Arabic scholars the last century has produced there are only two in England that rank with Edward Pococke on the same level—two men whose names stand out in bold relief, namely, Edward William Lane, prince among lexicographers, and William Wright, the brilliant exponent of the theories of the native Arabic grammarians.

The co-operation of Edward Pococke, the father, in the edition of this book, "Philosophus autodidactus," was indeed the best recommendation. To Edward Pococke, the father, is due the honour of having discovered and unearthed this priceless gem of Arabic philosophical literature, whilst the son, "the worthy son of so great a father," undertook the task, by no means an easy one, of editing the Arabic text and furnishing it with a Latin translation. This Latin translation was undoubtedly for that time a praiseworthy performance; yet, considering the enormous strides Oriental science has made during the last centuries, and with all the new material at hand, we are to-day able to put the philological groundwork on a more solid basis.

In casting about for the work of an Arabian philosopher for the "Wisdom of the East" Series, I could not think of anything more engaging, more captivating, than this simple romance.

Unfortunately, for reasons of space, I could not give a translation in full, but I have given the most interesting parts. On the passages, however, which I had to leave out, I have dwelt at greater length in this Introduction. In the translation I have tried to preserve the *cachet*, the archaic flavour and spirit of the book.

The idea underlying the story is, as Ockley puts it, to show how human capacity may, unassisted by any external help, attain to the knowledge of the higher world, and so by degrees find out its dependence upon a superior Being, the immortality of the soul, and other questions of the highest importance. In short, it describes the gradual awakening of the soul, the evolution of an original mind from its first groping in the dark to the most dazzling heights of philosophical speculation.

The great charm of the book lies in its simplicity and ingenuousness; in its entire freedom from affectation of style; in the transparent lucidity of its exposition, which is in pleasant contrast with the ponderous works of other philosophical writers amongst the Arabs.

Yet with all its ingenuousness, what sustained power of thought, what depth of philosophical penetration!

Hayy Ibn Yokdhan—this prototype of Robinson Crusoe—truly a pathetic, yet inspiring figure!

The simple setting of a man, living a solitary life on an Island, entirely given up to meditation and introspection, is used by our author as an arena for the display of his philosophical views, which, in kaleidoscopic transformation, cover the whole range of wisdom of those times—astronomical, geographical, cosmographic, physiological,—and so on, the whole picture touched with the wand of the master.

The author of the story, Ibn Tufail, though he is generally not reckoned among the most prominent in that brilliant array of Arabian philosophers for whom Spain became the rallying-point in the eleventh and twelfth centuries, yet his name will outlive centuries. For the romance which he has given to the world is a work of everlasting beauty, of immortal freshness; one that will never grow stale in the flight of ages.

Little is known of his private life, which seems to have passed by as uneventful as that of many of the philosophers and scientists of those ages.

He was born at Guadix, a little town of Andalusia. After having finished his education, he became a secretary at Granada, and later on we find him as Vezir and Physician to Abu Yakub, one of the first representatives of the dynasty of the Almohades. He died in Morocco, in 1185, leaving, besides his story of Hayy Ibn Yokdhan, only a few poems of insignificant value; whilst his principal work, the Self-taught Philosopher, has secured for him immortality.

In the following pages I will endeavour to give a short *résumé* of this story, though I am painfully aware of the fact that such an analysis can scarcely do justice to the beauty of the language nor to the wealth of philosophical thought and speculation represented therein.

From the outset the atmosphere is created with broad and happy touches.

On an Island in the Indian Ocean, famous for its health-giving atmosphere, abounding in fruits and inhabitants, Hayy Ibn Yokdhan comes into this world, as the son of a Princess, who is compelled to expose the child soon after his birth. The tide carries him to another Island, where he is found by a roe, that takes pity on him, nurses him like a mother, and watches over his every movement with tender affection.

Under her care he quickly develops into a fine strapping boy who is not afraid to venture a passage with wild beasts that dare to oppose him.

After the death of the roe, at which he is grief-stricken, he is wholly thrown on his own resources. Yet he knows how to look after himself. He covers himself with leaves of trees, and finds out other ways to keep himself warm and protected.

As the repairing of the coverings of leaves was very troublesome, he had a design of taking the tail of some dead beast and wearing it himself; but when he perceived that all beasts avoided those which were dead of the same kind, it made him doubt whether it was safe or not. At last, by chance he found a dead eagle, and observing that none of the beasts showed any aversion to that carcase, he concluded that this would suit his purpose, and so he cuts off the wings, the tail, and spreads the feathers open: then he draws off the skin and divides it into two equal parts, one of which he wears upon his back; with the other he covers his breast: the tail he wore behind and the wings were placed upon each arm.

This dress answered different ends: for in the first place it covered his nakedness, helped to keep him warm, and then it made him so frightful to the beasts that none of them cared to meddle with him or come near him.

After awhile he began to make experiments with the body of the roe, anxious to find out its composition.

He noticed, when he shut his eyes or held anything before him, he could see nothing at all till this obstacle was removed; and so, when he put his fingers in his ears that he could not hear till he took them out again. From which he concluded that all his senses and actions were liable to obstacles and impediments, upon the removal of which the same functions returned to their former course.

Now, when he found no visible defect in the external parts of the body of the roe, and yet at the same time perceived a universal cessation of its motions, he began to imagine that the hurt from which the roe had died was hidden in the inward part of the body.

Now he had observed on the bodies of wild beasts and other animals that all their members were solid, and that there were only three cavities, viz. the skull, the breast, and belly. He imagined, therefore, that the part the nature of which he wanted to find out must be in one of these cavities, and he had a strong persuasion that it was in the middlemost of them.

And having by this way of reasoning assured himself that the disaffected part lay in the breast, he resolved to open the breast of the roe; and, providing himself with sharp flints and splinters of dry cane almost like knives, he made an incision between the ribs, and, cutting through the flesh, came to the *Diaphragm.*

When he found this tough and not easily broken, he assured himself that such a covering must belong to that part for which he was looking out. After great efforts he succeeded in breaking through, and the first part he met was the lungs; and at last he found the heart, which he saw closed with a very strong cover and fastened with strong ligaments and guarded with a membrane.

On finding the same membrane on the inside of the ribs, and the lungs in the same posture as on the other side which he had opened first, he concluded the heart to be the part he looked for. When, however, he found that the being which had dwelt there before, had left its house before it fell to ruin, and forsaken it, the whole body seemed to him an inconsiderable thing.

Then his mind was perplexed with a variety of thoughts as to its substance and subsistence, the reason of its departure, etc. After much deliberation, at last he found that from that part of the heart which had departed proceeded all those actions by which the roe had shown her care of him and her affection,—that the body was only as an instrument or tool, like his cudgel with which he used to fight with the wild beasts. Thus all his regard for the body was over and transferred to that by which the body is governed, and by whose power it moves. So he decides in the end to bury the body.

After its burial, the impression of his loneliness and of his dependence upon himself being deepened, he quickly develops his faculties. In a short time he becomes an expert in different sports, as hunting and fishing. He makes himself clothes and shoes of the skins of wild beasts. By the observations he made upon the swallows' nests, being taught the art of building, he builds with his hands a room for his own use, a store-house, and a pantry. Then he contrives to make some wild horses so tractable that he can use them for riding, which is a great help to him in his expeditions and excursions.

His material existence thus once firmly established and secured, he begins to indulge in his speculations on all sorts of bodies,—on the different kinds of animals, plants, minerals and different sorts of stones, earth, water, exhalations and vapours, ice, snow, hail, smoke, fire, etc.

By the time he attains to the age of twenty-eight (fourth Septenary), his mind starts to ponder over astronomical problems—over heaven and stars, sun and moon; and in the end comes to the conclusion that the body of heaven is finite and is of a spherical figure.

At last his mind finds itself occupied with the great problem of Creation and Creator. With admirable skill the author delineates here the gradual development of Hayy's reasonings on the Creator and Mover of the world, and concludes with the panegyric words of the Koran: *He is the Existence, He is the Absoluteness, He is the Perfection, He is the Beauty, He is the Glory, He is the Power, He is the Knowledge, He is He, and all Things perish beside Him.*

All his thoughts were henceforward confined to the contemplation of this necessarily self-existent Being. In order to do this, he removed all his affections from sensible things, shut his eyes, stopped his ears, and refrained himself as much as possible from following his imagination, endeavouring to the utmost to think of nothing besides him.

Whilst so, on the one side, the imagination and all the other faculties which make any use of the organs of the body grew weak; on the other side, the operations of his essence which did not depend upon the body grew strong, so that sometimes his meditation was pure and free from any mixture, and he beheld thereby the necessarily self-existent Being; but then again corporeal faculties would return upon him and spoil his contemplation, and bring him down to the lowest degree.

Thus he continued, he opposing his corporeal faculties, and they opposing him, and mutually struggling one against another. Then, when he observed that the negative attributes consisted in separation from bodily things, he began to strip himself of all bodily properties—to remove and reject all those things from himself, as being in no wise consistent with that state which he was now in search of.

Thus he continued, confining himself to rest in the bottom of his cave, with his head bowed down and his eyes shut, and turning himself altogether from all sensible things and the corporeal faculties, and turning all his thoughts and meditations upon the *necessarily self-existent Being* without admitting anything else besides him: and if any other object presented itself to his imagination, he rejected it with his utmost force, and persisted therein to that degree that sometimes he did neither eat nor stir for many days together.

When he succeeded in preventing the admission of an extraneous object into that contemplation, he endeavoured as it were to disappear from himself—to detach himself entirely from his corporeal faculties, so as to be wholly taken up in the vision of that true Being.

And, thereto when at last he attained both the heaven and the earth, all spiritual forms and corporeal faculties, and all those powers that are separate from matter, all disappeared and vanished, and were as if they had never been. And amongst these his own being disappeared too, till at last there remained nothing but this *One, True, Perpetually Self-existent Being,* who spoke thus in that saying of his (the Koran): To whom now belongs the Kingdom? To this One, the Almighty God.

Thus he deeply immersed himself into this state, and witnessed "that which neither eye hath seen, nor ear heard, nor hath it ever entered into the heart of man to conceive."

When he came to himself from that state which was like drunkenness—he began to think that his own essence did not at all differ from the essence of that True Being, and that there was nothing in him but this true essence. It appeared to him that this True, Powerful, and Glorious Being was not by any means capable of multiplicity, and that his knowledge of his essence was his very essence, from whence he argued thus: "He that has the knowledge of this essence, has the essence itself, but I have the knowledge of this essence. Ergo, I have the essence itself."

Now Hayy Ibn Yokdhan being wholly immersed in the speculation of those things, and perfectly abstracted from all other objects, saw in the highest sphere a Being devoid of any maker; it was like the image of the sun which appears in a well-polished looking-glass. In the essence of that separate sphere he saw such perfection, splendour, and beauty, as is too great to be expressed by any tongue and too subtle to be clothed in words. It was, as he perceived it, in the utmost perfections of delight and joy, exaltation of gladness.

The next sphere to it—that of the fixed stars, had an immaterial essence that was not the essence of that *True one*, nor the essence of that highest, separated sphere, nor the sphere itself, but like the image of the sun that is reflected upon a looking-glass from another glass placed opposite to the sun; and in this essence he observed also the like splendour, beauty, loveliness, and pleasure that he had observed in the essence of the other highest sphere; the same splendour and delight he saw also in other essences. In fact, in all the spheres he observed immaterial distinct essences of the same kind; he saw such beauty, splendour, pleasure, and joy as eye has not seen nor ear heard, until he came to the lower world, subject to generation and corruption, which comprehends all that is contained within the sphere of the moon.

This essence, immaterial like the rest, had seventy thousand faces, and every face seventy thousand mouths, and every mouth seventy thousand tongues, that sanctified and glorified incessantly that One, True Being.

Now, he perceived in his own essence, and in those other ones that were in the same rank with him, infinite beauty, brightness, and light, such as neither eye has seen nor ear heard, nor has it entered into man's heart, which none can describe nor understand, but those which have attained thereto, and know it by experience.

But, on the other hand, he saw a great many other immaterial essences that resembled rusty looking-glasses, covered over with filth, and having their faces marked from those polished looking-glasses that had the image of the sun imprinted upon them. These essences had so much filthiness adhering to them, and such manifold defects, as he could not have conceived. Besides they were afflicted with infinite pains, that caused incessant sighs and groans; they were compassed with torments and "scorched with the fiery veil of separation."

Then, when he came to consider the divine essences and heroic spirits, he found them to be free from body and all its adherents, and removed from them at the utmost distance, having no connection or dependence upon them; their sole connection and dependence being that *One True Necessary Self-existent Being* who is the beginning and the cause of their existence.

Now, though the sensible world follows the divine world as a shadow does the body, and the divine world stands in no need of it and is independent of it; yet, it is absurd to suppose a possibility of its being annihilated, because it follows the divine world: but the corruption of this world consists in its being changed, not annihilated. And that glorious book (the Koran) spoke, where is no mention made of "moving the Mountains and making them like the world, and men like fire-flies, and darkening the Sun and Moon; and eruption of the Sea in that day when the earth shall be changed into another earth and the heavens likewise."

This is the substance of what Hayy saw when in his glorious state of ecstasy.

When *Hayy*, after his digression into the higher world, returned to the sensible world, he began to loathe the troubles of this mortal life on earth, and became very anxious to return to the same state he had been in before.—And by dint of continued exercise and strenuous endeavour he was at last able to attain to that state whenever his desire drove him to do so. While in this state he wished that God might detach him altogether from his body and bodily desires and necessities, so that he might give himself up for ever to his delight, and be freed from all grief and pain.

In the meantime he had passed the *Seventh Septenary*, and had attained to the age of fifty. And then came suddenly the great metamorphosis in his life, viz. his connection and acquaintanceship with another human being, called *Asal.*

This came about in the following way:

Not very far from the Island where Hayy passed his days, there was another Island to which had retired one of those pious sects which abounded then in that part of the world. Among its votaries were the most zealous and devoted members, two men, named Asal and Salaman. Though both were constant in performing those ceremonies prescribed by the law of this sect, they greatly differed in their character and in their propensities.

Asal, being of a contemplative and meditative disposition, affected retirement from the world and a solitary life as the best means to attain to happiness and salvation. *Salaman*, on the other hand, with his natural aversion to contemplation, and subtle inquiries into the higher world of things, preferred conversation, human society, and company, as the best means to drive away evil thoughts. Though they were the best of friends, this disparity in their views caused them in the end to separate.

Asal, advised of the fertility and health-giving atmosphere of that Island wherein *Hayy Ibn Yokdhan* dwelled, decided to go thither. After having sold his goods, and having distributed part thereof among the poor, he hired a ship and was transported into Hayy's Island.

As *Hayy*, being wholly taken up in sublime speculations, scarcely ever stirred out of his cave, Asal did not at first light upon him. One day, however, when Hayy was stepping out of his cell to look out for some food, he spied *Asal*—and the following episode forms one of the most charming chapters of the story in its description of how Hayy brings Asal to book, and how they try to make themselves understood to one another.

Hayy, who is taken by *Asal* to be one of those religious persons given to solitude, like himself, who had retired to that Island to give himself up to contemplation and prayers, stands, on his part, in wonder and amazement at the appearance of *Asal*. He could not imagine what it was. For of all the creatures he had ever beheld in his life, there was none that in the least resembled him. And in the end he came to the conclusion that he must be one of the essences, that had the knowledge of the True One. He is anxious to get into closer contact with him; and therefore, when he sees Asal making off with all might and in great haste, he follows him, and, being endowed with great bodily vigour, overtakes him, seizes him, and holds him fast so that he could not get off again.

When *Asal* looked upon him, and beheld him clothed with the skins of wild beasts, and his own hair so long that it covered part of his body, he felt great fear of him and tried to pacify him by stroking him. *Hayy*, on the other hand, when he perceived those tokens of his fear, endeavoured to allay it with such vocal expressions as he had learned from some animals, and furthermore by stroking, with great gentleness, his hand, his head, his neck, until he succeeded, by the expression of great kindness and joy, in allaying *Asal's* fears.

Then *Asal*, being a great expert in languages, began to question him concerning his doings and ways of life in all the languages he was master of. But *Hayy* did not understand anything of all that was said to him; and so they stood for a long time, wrapped up in wonder, looking at one another.

Asal, however, did not lose hope that it should come to pass that he should teach him languages, knowledge, and religion; and by dint of patience and application, he at last succeeded in teaching him the rudiments of language; and then he very quickly advanced him so far that he could converse with him any length of time.

Thereupon, he began to question him about his past and about his manner of living, and *Hayy* described to him the progress he had made in knowledge until he had attained to that degree of union with God, and told him of those essences that are separated from the sensible world; and of that essence, the True One, the Almighty and Glorious, with all his glorious attributes.

When *Asal* heard of all this, the eyes of his heart were opened and his mind enlightened, and he realised that all those rules and precepts he had been taught himself in his law, regarding the Almighty and Glorious God, his Angels and Books, his Messengers and the Day of Judgment, Paradise and Hell, were, in fact, resemblances of what Hayy had seen, and that his religion and Hayy's philosophy were only two different forms of the One Eternal Truth.

Now, when *Hayy* heard from *Asal*, in the course of their further conversations and discussions, of the sad state of the inner life which the people on *Asal's* Island lived in, he was greatly affected with pity towards them, and a resolution entered into his mind of going over to them in the hope and desire to become an instrument in their salvation. *Asal* quickly fell in with this plan. So they took the first ship that passed the shore of their Island and repaired to the opposite Island.

When they arrived there, *Asal's* friends gathered round him, anxious to hear of his adventures; and when they heard his account of *Hayy Ibn Yokdhan*, they flocked together from all sides, surrounding him with all tokens of reverence and admiration.

Hayy sets to work at once. He begins to explain to them the mysteries of wisdom, and to inculcate them with those precepts with which he was imbued. But as they were diametrically opposed to the notions deeply rooted in their minds, they began to withdraw themselves from him, and to loathe and abhor him; outwardly, however, in his presence, making a great show of kindness.

Hayy soon found out that it was hopeless to reform these people, whose only God was their lusts and appetites, blinded and captivated as they were by the trifles and vanities of this world, tossed up and down until they tottered to their graves. He saw that God had sealed up their hearts and ears, a thick mist being before their eyes and sore punishment abiding them.

When Hayy saw how things stood—that there was no salvation for this weak, tractable, and defective sort of men, he craved pardon for the things he had spoken and desisted from further efforts in that direction.

Greatly disappointed at being unable to regenerate Salaman's subjects, he bade him farewell and returned with Asal to his Island. There they continued to devote themselves to contemplation and the search after the Eternal Truth, and did not cease worshipping God until death laid his hands upon them.

These are the outlines of the story of Hayy Ibn Yokdhan.

Both Myth and History are the parents of many of its most touching and tender motives.

Stranded, or rather exposed on an Island by his mother, a Princess—who is not reminded of the same motive in a biblical story?—nursed by a Roe—another favourite motive of semi-mythical periods.

Later on, wholly left to his own resources, yet nothing daunted, by sheer pluck and energy he builds himself up a material existence, then by the sharpness of his wit, the originality and penetration of his thought, the incisiveness of his intuition, he rapidly builds up a spiritual structure of Nature, Heaven, and its Mover and Ruler, God, until, at the age of fifty, he has attained to that highest stage of Sufic evolution, the Ecstasy, the complete immersion in, and absorption by, the One Essence, the True One, that Eternal Being: Ecstasy, the same state which is so beautifully described by that famous Arabian philosopher, Avicenna, when he says:—"Then when a man's desires are raised to a high pitch, and he is sufficiently well exercised in that way, there will appear to him some small glimmerings of the Truth, as it were flashes of lightning, very delightful, which just shine upon him and then go out. Then the more he exercises himself, the more often he'll perceive them . . . till through frequent exercise he at last attains to a perfect tranquillity: and that which used to appear to him only by fits and starts, becomes habitual; and that which was only a glimmering before, a constant light."

To detach and deliver the soul—if only for a few hours—from the withering despotism of everyday life and strife, grey and monotonous with its eternal round of toil, worry, and trouble; to bathe the soul in the full sunshine of sublime wisdom, depicted and represented in this simple romance, with its exquisite charm and captivating grace, clear as crystal yet pregnant with ideas that have moved the world—this was the idea which guided me in embarking upon this work.

If I have succeeded in this task, even only in a small degree, by resuscitating this gem of Arabian philosophical literature—then I consider myself richly repaid for the labour I have bestowed on this little book, which has, indeed, been a labour of love.

PAUL BRÖNNLE.

25th April 1904.

This book, by the way, was the first book in Arabic type which issued from the Oxford University Press, just as his "Porta Mosis," containing the six Prefatory Discourses of Maimonides on the Mishna, was the first Hebrew text (in fact Arabic with Hebrew characters) printed at Oxford.

The value of the book was quickly recognised. In a comparatively short time it quite caught the fancy of the public—in fact it took the world by storm, and for a long time it remained greatly in vogue.

THE AWAKENING OF THE SOUL
A PHILOSOPHICAL ROMANCE.

Different Accounts of the Birth of Hayy Ibn Yokdhan.

Our good Forbears—may God be gracious unto them—report: there is an Island amongst the Indian Islands (in the Indian Ocean), situated under the Equinoctial, where men spring into being without father or mother. There is also planted a tree that produces women, and they are those whom al-Masʿudi calleth the Wakwak Damsels.

The Island is so blessed with the influence of light and sun as to be the most temperate and perfect of places; an opinion, however, that does not agree with that of the greatest philosophers and most famous physicians, who hold that there is nothing more temperate in the world than the fourth climate. According to them Hayy Ibn Yokdhan belonged to the number of those that are born without father or mother. Others, however, relate the story in a different manner. They tell us:

Hayy Ibn Yokdhan, son of a Princess.

Not far from this Island there lay another Island of great tract and large compass, abounding in fruits and well peopled. It was then governed by a Prince of haughty, fierce, and jealous disposition: he had a sister, graced with matchless beauty. He kept her in close custody and would not permit her to marry; for among her suitors there was not one he declared worthy of her.

Yet in spite of his watchfulness, his near kinsman, named Yokdhan, succeeded in winning her affections, and married her clandestinely according to the rites commonly known in those times. And before long she was with child and delivered of a son.

Hayy is exposed by his Mother.

Being in fear lest the matter should be discovered and her secret disclosed, she put him into a little ark and closed it firmly after having suckled the babe. Accompanied by her most trusted servants, she carried it to the seashore early in the night, her heart burning and distracted with love and fear, and then (tenderly kissing him with tearful eyes) she took her last leave of him, sending up this prayer to God:—

"O God! thou didst create this little child, when as yet it was nothing; thou didst cherish and nourish him while he lay confined within the dark closet of my womb; thou didst take great care of him until he formed into perfection and harmony. I, trembling before the haughty, unjust, and violent Prince, commend him unto thy goodness and pray that thou who surpasseth all in mercy wilt be bountiful unto him. Be thou, I pray thee, a guide and assistance unto him; forsake him not, and never leave him destitute of thy care."

Hayy is driven by the tide to another Island.

With these words she committed the little ark with the child into the sea, and the waters swelling with the tide carried it in the same night to the shore of another Island whereof we have just made mention.

It so happened that there was such a powerful current of the high water—as it does happen there once a year—that the ark was carried right to the shore, and by its force cast into a shady grove, thick set with trees,—a very pleasant place, well sheltered from wind and rain, and secured from the sun, which at its rising and setting receded from it.

Then when the waters subsided, the ark wherein the infant peacefully slumbered was left stranded, banked up by sands, safely aground, sheltered from blustering wind or in-coming tide. For when the wind blew, the sands were heaped together and obstructed the passage to the grove, and thus prevented the coming of any water into it so that the flood could not reach it.

Hayy is found by a Roe, which takes care of him.

Now it came to pass that the nails of the ark and its joints became loosened by the violence of the waves. The child, feeling hungry, began to cry bitterly, seeking relief and moving about in the ark. Fortunately it so happened that its cry was heard by a roe that was wandering about in search of her fawn, which, having ventured out of its den, had been carried off by an eagle.

When she heard the cry, she at first took it to be the cry of her fawn; so she followed it quickly up, until she came to the ark. She at once started to break it open with her hoofs, and, aided by the struggling child within, she at last forced a board covering the upper part of the ark.

Whereupon, beholding the dear child, she took pity on him, and being moved with tender affection towards him, she suckled him. Thus she fully satisfied him with milk, and, while he was weak and helpless, did come and guard him, defending him from evil and keeping him from all harm. And this is the tale that is told by those who refuse to believe that a man can come into the world without parents. But we shall explain later on how it grew and how it progressed until it reached unto great perfection.

Spontaneous Generation.

Those, however, who think he was born out of the earth, without father or mother, say that, in a low piece of ground in that Island, it happened that in the course of years a certain mass of clay so fermented that the four qualities heat and cold, moisture and dryness, agreed in equal mixture and in equal strength; and there was a great bulk of this clay in which some parts excelled the others, being more equally tempered and therefore fitter for the generation (of a mixed body); the middle portion of the clay being of the most perfect temper, and most closely approaching the human temper. The matter being in a state of fermentation, bubblings arose by reason of its great clamminess; and it came to pass that there was some clammy thing in the midst of it with a small bubbling, being divided with a thin partition into two parts, full of a spirituous and airy body, of the most equal temper. Thereupon, at the command of the most high God, a spirit was infused into it and joined so closely thereto that it could scarcely be separated therefrom either by sense or thought; this spirit constantly flowing out from God, as is manifest in the light of the sun which constantly influenceth the world . . . and creates.

Hayy grows up nursed by the Roe.

According to the other account (which we follow) the infant developed and grew, being nourished with the roe's milk, until he was two years old. By this time he began to walk by degrees and grow his foreteeth. He always followed the roe, who guarded him with most tender affection, and led him into places where there grew trees full of fruit, and fed him with ripe and sweet fruits that fell from the tree, breaking those that had a hard shell with her teeth.

She suckled the babe whenever he pleased. When he thirsted for water, she led him thereto; when the beams of the sun were in any way troublesome to him, she shaded him. When he suffered from the cold, she cherished and warmed him. And when the night approached, she brought him home to his former abode and covered him with her own body and partly with feathers such as remained of those wherewith the ark was stuffed when he was first put into it. When they went forth in the morning or came home of an evening, they were always accompanied by a herd of deer that lay together with them, in the same place.

Hayy learns to imitate animals' voices.

In this way the boy keeping company with them also learned their voice, which he imitated so exactly that scarcely any difference could be perceived between them. In like manner, whatever other voice he heard, whether of bird or beast, he came very near it by virtue of a very apprehensive faculty wherewith he was endowed. But of all the voices he imitated, he made most use of the deer's when they cried out for help or called their fellow-deer, when they wanted them nearer by or farther off. For as you know, those creatures have diverse voices according to their various ends and uses. Thus the child kept company with the deer, and they were not in the least afraid of one another.

Hayy begins to take a careful view of things.

Now when the images of things, after being removed out of sight, became fixed in his mind, it affected him so that he took a fancy to some things, whilst he had a distaste for others. In the meanwhile he took a careful view of all the beasts. He saw them covered with wool, hair, and different kinds of plumes; he beheld their great swiftness and strength and the weapons they were armed with for protection and defence, viz. horns, teeth, hoofs, spurs, nails, and the like. Then he viewed himself and found he was naked, destitute of weapons, slow and weak. For whenever they contended with him about the fruits they were to feed on, he generally got the worst of it; they pulled the fruit from him, keeping it for themselves, and he could not beat them off or flee from them.

Hayy observes the difference between the animals and himself.

Moreover, he observed that his fellow-fawns began to have little horns which they had not had at first; and while they were at first weak, and unable to run far, yet in progress of time grew to be very vigorous and nimble, and active in their movements. But none of all this he perceived to befall himself, and as often as he pondered over the matter, he could not make out what should be the reason thereof.

Also, when he beheld the creatures such as had any fault or defect of limbs, he could not find one amongst them like himself. All these matters evoked great grief and anxiety within him; and after having earnestly pondered over the matter and perplexed himself therewith, he at last gave up, in utter despair, the hope of being supplied with that, the want of which so sorely troubled his mind.

Hayy as a boy of seven. He covers himself with leaves.

Thereupon he, having by this time grown to be a boy of seven, decided to put forth his own efforts and to help himself. He took some broad leaves of trees (wherewith to cover his nakedness) and put some on the fore-part of his body, covering the hinder parts with the others; and having thus made a girdle of palm-leaves and rushes together, he girded his waist therewith.

But it was not long before the leaves, growing dry, withered and fell off from him.

Hayy, by no means discouraged, at once took fresh ones in their stead, and put them one on top of another, thus forming double folds; but even then, though remaining somewhat longer, they would not last but a short time. Thereupon, he broke off the bough of a tree, the ends whereof he made straight, stripping off the twigs, and then smoothed the middle parts thereof.

Hayy becomes aggressive, and attacks wild beasts.

Thus armed, he began to attack and affright such of the wild beasts as ventured to oppose him, assaulting the weaker and defending himself against the stronger. In this way he came to understand to some degree his own strength, and found out that his head by far excelled theirs, as he had been enabled therewith to cover his own nakedness and to provide himself with a weapon wherewith to defend himself. So that now he had no need of those natural weapons which he had formerly so much desired.

Hayy covers himself with the skin of an Eagle.

By this time he had grown up and was now past seven years of age; and as he found the frequent repairing of the leaves wherewith he covered himself very troublesome to him, it entered his mind to take unto him the tail of some dead beast, and gird it about him. But when he noticed that all the beasts shunned the dead bodies of those that were of the same kind, and saw them flee from them, he began to feel doubtful whether it was safe for him to do so, until at length he lighted one day on a dead eagle; and when he noticed that none of the animals fled before him, he thought that from him he might get his desire accomplished.

So, seizing the opportunity, he stepped forward towards him and first cut off the wings and the tail complete just as they were; then he smoothed the feathers, and spread them open; thereupon he tore off the remainder of the skin, dividing it into two portions, whereof he wore the one on his back, the other upon his belly and the secret parts. The tails he fixed behind and the wings on his arms. Thus he was at the same time covered and kept warm.

Hayy spreads terror among the beasts.

Moreover, he spread such terror among the beasts that they did not venture to resist or oppose him, and none dared to come near him except his roe which had suckled him and brought him up; and he never separated from her nor she from him. And when she became old and weakly, he led her to those places where there was the best food to be found, gathering the sweetest fruits and giving them to her to eat.

Hayy is grief-stricken at the death of the Roe.

Yet in spite of all the care he bestowed upon her, she grew more lean and feeble every day, and in the end death overtook her, when all her motions stopped and her actions ceased.

When the boy noticed this, sad grief overcame him, and he was stricken with the greatest sorrow. He called her with the same voice she used to answer; and though he shouted at the top of his voice, he could not perceive any movement or alteration in her. Thereupon he began to look closer into her eyes and ears, but could not find any visible defect. In equal manner, when he examined all the other parts of the body, he could find nothing amiss. He therefore earnestly desired to find out where the defect lay hidden, so that he might be able to remove it and make her return to her former state of vigorous life. But he was quite at a loss and utterly unable to find by what means to attain his ends. . . .

Hayy takes an aversion to the dead Body.

In the meantime the dead body of the roe began to putrefy and to exhale noisome vapours, which tended to increase his aversion to it and made him unwilling to look upon it.

Not long after this he chanced to see two ravens fighting together, and one of them struck the other down dead. After that it began to scrape the earth with its claws, till it had dug up a pit wherein it buried the carcase of its adversary. When Hayy observed this, he said to himself: "How well has this raven done in covering the body of his companion, though he did ill in killing him. How much greater reason was there for me to have performed this good office to my mother."

Hayy buries the body of the Roe.

Thereupon he digged a grave, in which he laid his mother's body, throwing earth upon it. Then he went on meditating on the thing which had governed the body, but could not apprehend what sort of thing it was. But when he looked on the rest of the roes, and saw that they all had the same figure and form as his mother had had, he gathered there was in every one of them something that governed and actuated them, like that which had actuated and governed his mother. And on account of that likeness he continued to follow them, and liked to be in their company.

Hayy observes divers kinds of Living Creatures and Plants.

In this condition he remained some time, contemplating divers kinds of living creatures and plants, and walking about the shore of that Island to see whether he could find anything like himself, as he observed many of the other animals and plants had many resembling one another. But as much as he looked about, he could not find one like himself. And when, on walking round, he perceived that the Island was everywhere compassed with the sea, he fancied there was no other Island besides.

Hayy discovers Fire kindled by the friction of Reeds.

But once it so happened that fire was kindled by friction among a parcel of reeds, which at first greatly frightened him, being a thing he had never seen before, so that he stood at a distance a good while, greatly wondering at it.

Yet at last he ventured to draw nearer and nearer to it by degrees; in amazement he observed the brightness of its light, and that wondrous force in consuming everything it seized, converting it into its own nature, till in the end, full of wonder and incited by that innate boldness and courage that God had implanted in his mind, he felt induced to stretch his hand out to get hold of it.

But when it burnt his fingers, and he saw he could not lay hold of it, he endeavoured to take a stick from the burning tree which the fire had not as yet completely seized upon, and taking hold of that part that was still untouched, he easily gained his ends and carried the tree brand home to his lodgings, which he had selected.

There he kept his fire and ceased not to tend it day and night. Particularly at night it was of great service to him, inasmuch as its light and heat supplied the place of the sun, so that he was greatly pleased with it and began to look upon it as the most excellent thing he had yet had about him.

And when he noticed that it always tended upwards—he felt convinced that it was one of those celestial substances which he saw shining in the firmament. He then tried the strength thereof upon all sorts of bodies by throwing them into it, and he perceived it consumed them all sooner or later according to their natures, which rendered them more or less combustible.

Amongst other experiments wherewith he tried to prove its strength, he flung therein certain fishes which the sea had cast upon the shore; as the steam thereof came to his nose, the smell whetted his appetite so that he ventured to taste of them; and when he found it agreeable to his palate, he began to get used to the eating of fish and flesh. Then he applied himself to fishing and hunting those creatures that are specially fit to feed on, until he became a great expert in those sports.

Thus his regard for the fire greatly increased day by day, because it helped to provide him with various sorts of food with which he was quite unacquainted before.

THE THIRD SEPTENARY

Hayy makes himself Clothes and Shoes of the Skins of Animals.

By the time he had attained to the end of his *third septenary*, viz. to the twenty-first year of his age, he had found out many things which were of great use to him for the conveniences of life. He made himself clothes and shoes of the skins of wild beasts after he had dissected them for use. He made himself thread of their hair, as also of the rind of the stalks of althea mallows, and other plants that could be easily parted asunder and drawn into threads. And he learned the making of these threads from the use he had made of the rushes before. He made a sort of bodkin of the strongest thorns he could get and splinters of cane sharp pointed with stones.

The art of building he was taught by the observations he made upon the swallows' nests. He built himself a room to repose and rest therein, and also a store-house and pantry to lay up the remainder of his victuals. He guarded it with a door made of canes twisted together to prevent any of the beasts from getting in when he happened to be away. He also got hold of certain birds of prey which he made use of for hawking, and others of the tamer sort which he bred up, and fed upon their eggs and chickens. He also took to him the horns of wild bulls, which he fastened upon the strongest canes he could get and the staves of the tree Alzan and others of similar kind.

Thus, by the help of fire and of sharp edged stones, he so fitted them that they served him as spears. He made himself also a shield of the skins of beasts folded and compacted together. And thus he tried to provide himself with artificial weapons, being destitute of natural arms.

Hayy learns to ride.

When he saw that his hand supplied all those defects quite well, and that none of the various kinds of wild beasts ventured to stand up against him, but fled away from him and only excelled him in their swiftness, he bethought himself of contriving some art how to be even with them, and finally decided there would be nothing so convenient as to chase some of the strongest and swiftest beasts of the Island, nourishing them with food until they might let him get on the back of them, so that he might pursue other kinds of wild beasts.

There were in that island wild horses and asses, out of which he chose some that seemed fittest for the purpose, and by dint of exercise he made them so tractable that he became complete master of his wishes. And when he had made out of the skins of those beasts something that served him instead of bridles and saddles, it was an easy matter for him to overtake such beasts, which he scarcely could have taken in any other way.

He made all these discoveries whilst he busied himself in the study of anatomy, studiously searching after the properties of the component parts of animals and their difference, and all this he did, as we mentioned above, by the time he was twenty-one years of age.

Hayy examines the Nature of Bodies.

After this he proceeded further to examine the nature of bodies that were subject to generation and corruption, as the different kinds of animals, plants, minerals and different sorts of stones, earth, water, exhalations and vapours, ice, snow, hail, smoke, fire, and hoar-frost.

In all these he observed different qualities and a diversity of actions and motions, agreeing in some respects and differing in others. He found that, so far as they agreed, they were *one*; where they disagreed, *a great many*; and when he looked into the properties whereby they were distinguished from one another, he found them so manifold that he could not comprehend them.

As to himself, he knew that his spirit was one in essence, and was really the substance of his being, and that the other parts served only as so many instruments. So he perceived his own essence to be but one.

Then attentively considering the different kinds of animals, he perceived that the one thing common to them all was sensation and nutrition and the faculty of moving of their own accord wheresoever they pleased, all of which actions he was assured were the proper effects of the animal spirit, and that those lesser things in which they differed were not so proper to that spirit.

For he considered that the animal spirit may differ with regard to some qualities, according to the variety of constitutions in several animals. And so he looked upon the whole species of living creatures as one.

Then, on contemplating the different species of plants, he perceived that the individuals of every species were like one another in their boughs, branches, leaves, fruits; and so, taking a view of all the different kinds of plants, he decided within himself that they were all *one* and the same in respect of that agreement between themselves in their actions, viz. their nourishment and growth.

He then contemplated those bodies which have neither sense, nourishment, nor growth, such as stones, earth, water, air, and fire; which he saw had all of them three dimensions, viz. *length*, *breadth*, and *thickness*; and that their differences only consisted in this, that some of them were coloured, others not; some were hot, others cold, and similar differences.

He noticed also that hot bodies grew cold, and, on the contrary, cold ones grew warm. He saw further that water rarefied into vapours, and vapours again thickened and turned into water. Then he observed that the bodies which were burnt turned into coals, ashes, flame, and smoke; and that the smoke, when in its ascent it was intercepted by an arch of stones, thickened them into soot, and became like other earthly substances. From whence he concluded that all things were in reality *one*, like the animals and plants, though multiplied and diversified in some respects.

Hayy transfers his thoughts to the Heavenly Bodies.

Now after he had attained thus far, so as to have a general and indistinct notion of an *Agent*, a vehement desire seized him to get a more distinct knowledge of him. But since he had not yet withdrawn himself from the sensible world, he began to look for this voluntary Agent among things sensible; nor did he know, as yet, whether it were one Agent or many. Therefore he took a view of all the bodies that were near him, viz. which his thoughts had been continually fixed upon; which he found all successively liable to generation and corruption, either completely or in parts, as *water* and *earth*, parts of which are consumed by *fire*.

He perceived likewise that the air was changed into snow by extremity of cold, and then again into water; and among all the other bodies which he had near him, he could find none which had not its existence anew and required some voluntary Agent to give it a being. Therefore he laid all those sublunary bodies aside, and transferred his thoughts to the consideration of the heavenly bodies.

THE FOURTH SEPTENARY

Hayy ponders over Heaven and Stars.

Thus far had he arrived with his reflections about the *fourth septenary* of his age. He recognised that the heavens and all the stars contained therein were bodies, because they are extended according to the three dimensions: length, breadth, and thickness.

Then he began to ask himself whether their extension was infinite, whether they extended to an endless length and breadth, or whether they were circumscribed by any bounds and terminated by certain limits.

Hayy finds that the Body of Heaven is finite.

This problem continually occupied his mind. But soon, owing to the power of his reflection and the penetration of his thought, he perceived that the idea of an infinite body was an absurdity, an impossibility, a notion quite unintelligible. And he confirmed himself in this way of thinking by numerous arguments that presented themselves to his mind.

And when, by the singular sharpness of his wit, he had satisfied himself that the body of heaven was finite, he wanted to find out, in the next place, of what form it was and how it was limited by the superficies that compassed it round.

Hayy contemplates Sun, Moon, and Stars.

First of all he contemplated the sun, moon, and stars, and saw that they all rose in the East, and set in the West; and those lights which went right over his head described a greater circle, whilst those at a greater distance from the vertical point towards the North or South described the lesser circle. So that the least circles which were described by any of the stars were those two which went round the two poles, the one North, the other South, the last of which is the circle of the star Suhail (that is Canopus) and the circle Al-farkadani, which was next the northern.

And, since he lived in an island situated under the equinoctial line, all those circles cut the horizon at right angles and had alike reference to North and South, seeing both the poles appeared to him at once. He observed that when a star arose in a larger circle and another in a lesser, yet they both arose together and set at the same time, and he noticed it to be the case with all stars at all times.

Hayy concludes that the Heaven is of a spherical Figure.

Therefore, it was evident to him that the heaven was of a spherical figure.

In this he was further confirmed by observing the return of the sun, moon, and the other stars to the East after their setting; and also because they always appeared to him of the same proportion of magnitude when they arose, when they were in the midst of heaven, and when they set; for if their motions had not been circular, they must have been nearer to sight at some time than at others; and then their dimensions would have appeared greater or lesser when they were nearer to him or further off.

But since there was no such appearance, he felt assured that the figure of heaven was spherical. Then he considered the motion of the moon, and saw that it was carried from the East to the West as the other planets were. So that at length a great part of astronomy became known to him.

It appeared to him, further, that the motions of the planets were in different spheres, all of which were comprehended in another that was above them all, and which turned about all the rest in the space of a day and a night. But it would be too tedious to set down, to explain in particular, how he advanced in this science; and what we have already said is quite sufficient for our present purpose.

Now, when he had attained to this degree of astronomical science, he found that the whole of the heavens and whatever it contained was one thing composed of parts mutually joined together; and that all those bodies which he had before considered—as earth, water, air, plants, animals—were all of them contained in it, so that none of them went beyond its bounds. He found also that the whole body was like one animal in which the stars answered to the senses; the spheres joined together answered to the limbs; and all those bodies therein, which were liable to generation and corruption, resembled those things which are contained in the belly of an animal.

Hayy ponders over the Creation of the World.

Now, whereas it appeared to him that the whole world was only one Substance which stood in need of a voluntary Agent, and that its various parts seemed to him but one thing, in like manner as the bodies of the lower world which is subject to generation and corruption, he took a broad view of the whole world, and debated within himself whether it existed in time after it had been, and came to be out of nothing; or whether it was a thing that had existed from eternity and never wanted a beginning.

In respect to this matter, he had many and grave doubts within himself, so that neither of these opinions prevailed over the other. For when he proposed to himself the belief of eternity, there arose many objections in his mind with regard to the impossibility of an *infinite being*, just as the existence of an *infinite body* had seemed impossible to him.

He saw, furthermore, that any substance that was not void of *qualities* produced anew, but always endued with them, must also itself be produced anew, because it cannot be said to be before them; and that which cannot exist before qualities newly produced, must needs itself be newly produced.

On the other hand, however, when he proposed to himself to believe in a new production thereof, other objections occurred to him—in particular this, that the notion of its being produced after non-existence could in no wise be understood, unless it was supposed there was some time antecedent to its existence; whereas time was amongst the number of those things that belonged to the world and was inseparable therefrom, wherefore the world cannot be understood to be later than time.

He then reasoned within himself: if the world be produced anew, it must needs have a producer or creator; and if so, why did this creator create the world now and not before?

Was it because some motive supervened which it had not before? But there was nothing besides him, the Creator.

Was it, then, owing to some change in his own nature? If so, what has caused this change?

Thus he did not cease to consider these things within himself for some years, and to ponder over its different bearings; and a great many arguments offered themselves on both sides, so that neither of those opinions preponderated in his judgment over the other.

Hayy concludes that the world must have a Creator without bodily Substance.

Since it seemed difficult to him to make a definite decision on this question, he began to consider within himself what would be the necessary consequence which did follow from either of those opinions, and that they might both be alike. And he perceived that, if he supposed the world to be created in time, and to have had an existence after non-existence, it would necessarily follow therefrom that the world could not come forth into existence by its own power, but required some agent to produce it; but this agent could not be perceived by any of the senses; for if it were an object of the senses, it would be *body*, and if *body*, part of the world, and would have had its existence anew; so that it would have stood in need of some other cause which should have produced it anew. And if this second creator were also a body, he would depend upon a third, and that third upon a fourth, and so on *ad infinitum*, which, however, would be absurd and irrational.

The world, therefore, must necessarily have a creator that has not a bodily substance; and as the creator is, indeed, without such a bodily substance, it is quite impossible for us to apprehend him by any of our senses; for we perceive nothing by the help of the five senses but bodies or such qualities as adhere to bodies.

And since it cannot be apprehended by sense, neither can it be comprehended by imagination. For imagination is nothing else but a representation of the forms of things, when their bodily objects are absent. And seeing it is not a body, we must not attribute to him any bodily properties, the first of which is extension into length, breadth, thickness; but he is free from that, and also from all other properties of body that flow from it. And seeing he is the Creator of the world, doubtless he knows whatsoever is in it, and has the sovereign command over it. "Shall not he know, that created it? For he is most eminent in knowledge and omniscient." (Koran.)

On the other side he saw that if he believed in the eternity of the world, and that it was ever as it is now, and that no time of chaos preceded it, that necessarily it would follow that motion was from eternity also, without any period of beginning, because there could be no rest before it whence to take its beginning.

Now, every motion necessarily requires a *mover*, and that mover is either some power diffused in some body, to wit, either in the body of the thing moved or else through some other body without it, or else some other power that is not diffused or dispersed through anything at all.

Now every power diffused in any body and dispersed through it, is divided or doubled. For example: gravity in a stone which causes it to move downwards. For if the stone be divided into two parts, the gravity is also divided into two parts; and if you add thereto another stone of equal weight, the gravity is doubled. And if it were possible that the stone grew *ad infinitum*, the gravity would also grow *ad infinitum*. On the other hand, if the stone should grow to a certain size and remain there, also the gravity would increase to the same extent, and no farther.

Now it has already been demonstrated that every body must necessarily be finite, and consequently every power inherent in a body is also finite. If, therefore, we can find a power which produces an infinite effect, it must needs be such a power that is not inherent in any body.

Now we find that the heaven is moved with a perpetual motion, without any cessation at all.

Therefore, if we affirm that its motion has no beginning, it necessarily follows that the power that moves is not inherent in its own body nor in any other body that is without it; but proceeds from something altogether abstract from bodies, and which can be described by no terms applicable to bodies.

Then it was evident to him, from his former contemplation of the lower world which is liable to generation and corruption, that the true essence of body consisted in its form, which is its disposition to various motions, but that that part of its essence which consisted in matter was very mean and poor, and can scarcely be conceived. Therefore the existence of the whole world consists in its disposition to be moved by this Mover, who is free of all matter and of all adjuncts belonging to the body, abstracted from everything which senses can apprehend or imagination can reach.

And since he is the efficient cause of the motion of the heaven, in which (though there be different kinds) there is no difference, no innovation or cessation, doubtless he has power over it and a perfect knowledge of it.

Thus his contemplation brought him to the same conclusion to which he had arrived before. Nor did it trouble him in any way that he doubted the eternity of the world and its existence anew. For either way it was manifest to him that the Creator of the world was no body nor joined to body nor separated therefrom. For conjunction and separation, to be within and without, are the qualities of bodies, from which the Creator is quite free. And because every body stands in need of a form to be added to their matter, considering it cannot subsist but by that, nor exist without it, but by this voluntary Agent, it appeared to him that all things owed their existence to this Agent; and that none of them could subsist but through him; and consequently this Agent was the cause of them all, and they the effects, whether they were newly created after non-existence or whether they had no beginning with respect of time, without any privation foregoing it.

For upon either of these two cases their existence depended, for they could not continue, unless he continued, nor exist unless he existed, nor be eternal without his being eternal; but he stood not in any need of them nor in any way depended upon them.

And how should it be otherwise, considering it has been demonstrated that its power and virtue is infinite, whereas all bodies are finite and terminated and equally whatsoever adhereth unto them or dependeth upon them; therefore that the whole world, and whatsoever is in it, heaven, earth or stars, and whatsoever belongs to them, above or beneath them, is all his work and creation and consequently posterior to him in nature though not in time. As if you take any body in your hand and then move your hand, the body must necessarily follow the motion of your hand with a motion which is posterior to the motion of the hand in nature, though not in time, seeing both motions began together.

So all this world is created and caused by this Agent out of time, whose command is, when he would have anything done: *Let it be*, and *it is*.

Hayy admires the work of the Creator.

Now, when he saw that all things existing were the work of the Creator, he again considered the power of the same, greatly admiring so rare a workmanship, such accurate wisdom and profound knowledge.

There appeared to him in the most minute creatures (much more in the greater) such signs of wisdom and marvels of the work of creation that his mind was filled with the greatest admiration. Then he became assured that all these things must proceed from a voluntary Agent of infinite perfection, even above all perfection, to whom even the weight of an atom could not be unknown whether in heaven or earth, nor any other thing whether lesser or greater than it.

Thereupon he considered all the different sorts of animals, and how this Agent had given to every one of them such a fabric of body and then taught them what use to make thereof. For if he had not taught them to use the members he had given them for those employments for which they were designed, they would not have derived any benefit or advantage therefrom, but on the contrary would rather have found them a burden.

Hence he knew that he was most bountiful and most gracious of all. And then, when he perceived among the creatures anything that had beauty, perfection, power and strength, or whatever other excellency it had, he concluded that it must necessarily proceed from that voluntary Agent, from his existence and by his operation.

He knew that the qualities that were in him were much greater, more perfect, more absolute, more bountiful, more excellent and more lasting; and there was no comparison between those things that were in him and those that were found in the animals.

Nor did he cease to go on with his search till he had run through all the attributes of perfection, and found that they were all in the Agent and proceeded from him, and that he was worthy of them more than any to whom they should be ascribed.

Also he searched all the attributes of defects, and saw him free from them and void of them. And how was it possible for him to be otherwise, since the notion of imperfection is nothing but mere privation or what depends upon it.

How should he in any degree partake of privation, who is a most simple being, the very essence himself, and giving a being to everything that exists, and besides whom there is no existence. *For He is the Existence, He is the Absolute, He is the Perfection, He is the Beauty, He is the Glory, He is the Power, He is the Knowledge, He is He, and all Things perish beside Him.* (Koran.)

FIFTH SEPTENARY

Hayy is completely taken up with the Contemplation of the Superior Intellectual World.

Thus far he had advanced in his knowledge by the end of the *fifth septenary* from his birth, that is when he was thirty-five years old. And the consideration of this supreme being was then so fixed in his mind that it hindered him to think of any other thing, so that he forgot altogether the consideration of their existence and of their nature, until in the end it came to this, that as soon as he cast his eyes upon any thing of any kind whatsoever, he at once saw in it the prints of this Agent, and in a moment his thoughts were diverted from the Creature and transferred to the Creator, so that his heart was altogether withdrawn from thinking on this inferior world, which contains the objects of sense (inferior sensible world), and entirely taken up with the contemplation of the superior intellectual world.

Hayy examines all his Senses and Faculties.

Having now attained the knowledge of this supreme being of permanent existence, which has no cause of its own existence, but itself is the cause of the existence of all other things, he was next desirous to know by what means he came to this knowledge and by what faculty he had apprehended this being.

Therefore he first examined all his senses, viz. his hearing, seeing, smelling, tasting, and feeling, and saw that all these apprehended nothing but what was bodily or what is in the body.

For the hearing apprehended nothing but sounds, and these arose from the agitation of the air, by the friction of bodies. The sight apprehends colours, the smelling odours; the taste savours, the touch temperatures of the body, hardness and softness, roughness and smoothness. Nor does the imagination apprehend anything which has not length, breadth, and thickness.

Now all these things which are thus apprehended are the adjuncts of bodies, and our senses apprehend nothing else, because they are faculties diffused through our bodies and divided according to the division of bodies, and therefore cannot apprehend anything else but divisible body. For as this faculty is diffused through the visible body, it must necessarily, whenever it apprehends anything, be divided as the faculty is divided. Therefore every faculty which is seated in the body can apprehend nothing except a body, or what is inherent in a body.

Now it has already been shown that this necessarily existent being is free from all material qualities in any respect, and consequently cannot be apprehended except by something which is neither matter nor any faculty inherent in matter, or in any way dependent upon it, neither within it nor without it, neither joined to it nor separated from it.

It appeared also to him that he apprehended this supreme being, and that he gained a firm knowledge of it by that which was his own essence. It was therefore clear to him that his essence was something incorporeal without any material quality; and whatever material thing he apprehended by his outward sense, was not in reality his essence; but that it was something of an incorporeal substance, whereby he apprehended that absolute and perfect being that is necessarily and of itself existent.

Having thus learnt that his real essence was not a corporeal substance perceived by his senses and compassed about by his skin, his body seemed to him something altogether contemptible, and so he wholly addicted himself to the contemplation of that noble essence whereby he apprehended that noble and necessarily existent being. Then he considered within himself, whether this noble essence could possibly be dissolved, corrupted, and vanish altogether, or whether it were of perpetual duration.

Now he knew that corruption and dissolution were properties of bodies, and consisted in putting off one form and putting on another; as for instance when water is changed into air and air into water, or when herbs are turned into earth or ashes, and earth into herbs—for this is the true notion of corruption. But an incorporeal being, independent of body and altogether free therefrom, cannot be liable to corruption.

Having thus quite assured himself that his real essence could not be corrupted, he desired to know in what condition it would be itself when it left the body and was separated therefrom; but now he knew that it was not so, until the body was no longer a fit instrument for its use.

Therefore weighing in his mind all his apprehensive faculties, he saw that every one of them apprehended its object, sometimes potentially, sometimes actually—as when the eye is shut or turns itself away from the visible object, it is potentially apprehensive—which means, though it does not actually apprehend it at present, yet is able to do so for the time to come. And when the eye is open and turned toward the effect, it is actually apprehensive, which means, it apprehends it at present. And so it is with all the other faculties.

Furthermore he saw that if any of these faculties never actually apprehended its proper object, yet so long as it is potentially apprehensive, it has no desire to apprehend any particular object, because it has no knowledge thereof, as is seen in a man who is born blind. But if it did ever actually apprehend, and becomes afterwards potentially apprehensive, it is inclined to apprehend its object actually, because it has been acquainted with the object and is intent upon it, as a man, who has before enjoyed his sight, continually desires visible objects after he is blind; and the more glorious, perfect, and beautiful the object is, the more his desire increases and the greater is his grief for the loss.

So if we can find out anything which has an unlimited perfection, infinite beauty, brightness and splendour, that does not proceed from it, then he who is deprived of the sight and knowledge of that thing, after having once known it, must necessarily suffer inexpressible anguish, so long as he remains destitute thereof; whereas he that has it continually present before him, must needs enjoy uninterrupted delight, perpetual felicity, boundless joy and gladness.

HAYY RETURNS TO THE SENSIBLE WORLD.

As to the end of his story, I will tell you all about it, with the help of God.

When *Hayy* returned to the Sensible World, after his digression into the Divine World, he began to loathe the burden and troubles of this mortal life on earth, and to be filled with a most earnest and passionate desire of the life to come; and he strove to return to the same state in the same way as at first, until he attained thereto with less labour than he had done formerly. And he continued in it the second time longer than at the first.

Then he returned to the Sensible World; and then again he sought to re-enter into that state of speculation, and found it easier than the first and second time, and continued therein much longer.

In this way it grew easier and easier unto him, and his remaining therein became longer and longer, until at last he could attain it whenever he desired, and remain therein as long as he pleased, except when the necessity of his body required it. Those necessities, however, he had restrained within so narrow a compass that a narrower could hardly be imagined.

And, while in this state he often wished that God, the Almighty and Glorious, would altogether detach him from this body of his that called him away from that place, so that he might wholly and continually give himself up to his delight, and might be freed from all that pain and grief with which he was afflicted, as often as he was forced to turn his mind from that state to attend on his bodily necessities.

SEVENTH SEPTENARY

Asal and Salaman appear on the Scene.

Thus he continued in this state until he had passed the *seventh septenary* of his age, that is, until he was fifty years of age. Then it happened that he made the acquaintance of Asal. And the account of this meeting with him we shall now relate, with the help of God.

They report that there is an Island near unto that where *Hayy Ibn Yokdhan* was born—according to one of those two different accounts as to the manner of his birth—unto which had retired one of those pious sects that had for its founder some of the ancient Prophets (the Mercy of God be upon them!), a sect which used to discourse on all things that had a new existence in nature and by way of parables to represent their images to the imagination, so that their impressions fixed themselves in the minds of men. This sect spread itself in that Island and began to prevail and become famous, till at length the King himself entered it and forced his subjects also to adhere to it.

Now there were born in that same Island two men of great endowments and excellence, great lovers of goodness—their names were *Asal* and *Salaman*. Meeting with this sect, they embraced it most heartily, addressing themselves to the punctual observance of all its precepts and the continuous exercise of the works required thereby; and to that end they entered into a bond of friendship with each other. They studiously made careful inquiries into the passages contained in the law of that sect, amongst others on the descriptions of God, the Almighty and the most Glorious, and His angels; on the resurrection, and the rewards and punishments of a future life.

Nature and Character of Asal and Salaman.

Now, of the two *Asal* was the one who made a deeper search into the inside of things, was more given to studying mystical meanings and senses of words, and diligently endeavoured to interpret them. *Salaman*, on the other hand, his fellow student, mostly observed the outward things, never troubling himself about such interpretations, and abstained from a curious search and speculation of things. Apart from this difference, however, both were constant in performing those ceremonies prescribed, and strove to fight against their unruly passions and affections.

Further Differences of Asal and Salaman.

Now, in this law there were contained some sayings which seemed to exhort and encourage men to affect retirement and a solitary life, and to intimate that salvation and happiness were to be attained thereby; other sayings, again, seemed to encourage men unto conversation and fellowship and applying themselves to embrace human society.

Asal addicted himself wholly to retirement, and he preferred those sayings which tended thereunto, seeing that he was by nature inclined to perpetual contemplation, and searching into the meanings of things; for he had great hopes of attaining to his ends by selecting a solitary life.

Salaman, however, applied himself to conversation and human society and those sayings of the law that tended that way, because he had a natural aversion to contemplation and more subtle inquiries into things; and it occurred to him that society and company tended to drive away evil thoughts, and banished that diversity of opinions which intruded themselves into his mind and kept him from attending the motions and suggestions of evil spirits. And in the end their disagreement on this particular point caused them to depart one from another.

Asal repairs to Hayy's Island.

Now *Asal* had heard of that Island wherein it is reported that Hayy grew up. He knew the fruitfulness and conveniences thereof and the health-giving temper of its air, so that it would afford him such a resting-place as he wished to find. He decided, therefore, to go thither and to withdraw himself from company and society for the remainder of his days.

Therefore, gathering all his goods together, with a part thereof he hired a ship to convey him to that Island, whilst the rest he distributed among the poor people. Then he took his farewell from his friend Salaman and went abroad. The mariners transported him safely unto the Island, set him ashore, and departed.

There he continued serving God, the Almighty and Glorious, sanctifying him and meditating upon his glorious names and attributes, without being in any way interrupted or disturbed. When he felt hungry he took of the fruits of the Island or he got by hunting as much as satisfied his hunger.

In this state he remained for some time, enjoying the greatest possible pleasure and complete tranquillity of mind, arising out of the communication he had with his Lord; and every day experiencing his favours and most precious gifts, he easily brought to his hand such things as he wanted and were necessary for his support, which confirmed his belief in him and gave him great comfort.

Hayy Ibn Yokdhan in the meantime was wholly taken up with sublime speculations, and never stirred out of his cave but once a week, to take unto him such food as most readily presented itself. Thus it happened that *Asal* did not light upon him at first. For walking round the utmost parts of the

Island, and compassing the extremes thereof, he neither met any man nor could he perceive the footsteps of any one: which increased his gladness of mind, and he was delighted with what he had proposed unto himself—that was solitude and retirement.

Hayy and Asal meet.

At last it came to pass at a certain time that, *Hayy Ibn Yokdhan* stepping out of his cell to look out for some food in the same place to which *Asal* had retired, they spied one another.

Asal, for his part, had no doubt but that the man he saw was some religious person given to solitude who had retired into that Island as he had done himself. He was afraid, therefore, lest if he should come up to him and make himself known, it might spoil his meditation, and thus become an impediment to him in accomplishing his desires.

But, as for *Hayy Ibn Yokdhan*, he could not imagine what it was: for of all the creatures he had ever beheld in his life, there was none that resembled him in the least.

Now *Asal* was clothed in a black coat, made up of hair and wool, which he fancied was a natural cover; at which *Hayy* stood a long time in utter wonder and astonishment. Thereupon *Asal*, being afraid lest he should disturb his meditation and divert his attention therefrom, turned his back and fled. *Hayy Ibn Yokdhan* ran after him, driven by an innate desire to know and find out the truth of things.

When he saw, however, that *Asal* fled from him with all his might in such haste, he retired a little into the background and hid himself there, so that *Asal* thought he had gone off altogether and gone far away from that place where he had seen him. *Asal* therefore began to betake himself, as his custom was, unto his prayers and reading, to invocation and weeping, to supplication and complaining, and these exercises had quite turned him away from any other thing.

Hayy catches hold of Asal.

In the meantime *Hayy* drew near little by little, while *Asal* did not perceive him at all, until at length he came so near as to hear his reading and the prayers he uttered. He also took notice of his humble gesture and his weeping, whence he heard a pleasant voice, consisting of words quite distinct, such as he had never observed before in any kind of animals. Then, beholding his shape and lineaments, he observed that he was of the same form with himself. He was satisfied that the coat with which he was clothed was not a natural skin, but an artificial habit like unto his own clothing. And when he observed the decency and comeliness of his behaviour and his supplication and weeping, he did not at all question but that he was one of the Essences, which had the knowledge of the *True One.*

Therefore, he felt a passionate desire to get acquainted with him, to find out what was the matter with him and what was the cause of that weeping and supplication. Thereupon he came nearer unto him, until *Asal*, observing it, took to his heels again. But *Hayy Ibn Yokdhan*, endowed with vigour and power, both of knowledge and body, bestowed upon him by God—pursued him with all his might, till at last he overtook him, seized him, and held him fast that he could not make again his escape from him.

Hayy and Asal stroke one another.

Thereupon, when *Asal* looked upon him and beheld him clothed with the skins of wild beasts with the hair on, and his own hair so long that it covered part of his body, and observed his great swiftness and strength, he was greatly afraid of him and began to pacify him by stroking him, and to entertain him in words. But *Hayy Ibn Yokdhan* did not understand a word of what he said nor knew any of his meaning, only he perceived the tokens of his fear and endeavoured to allay his fear with such voices as he had learned from some of the animals: he gently stroked his hand, his head, and the sides of his neck, and showed kindness unto him and expressed much gladness and joy, till at last *Asal's* fear was assuaged, and he perceived that he intended no evil to him.

Hayy and Asal try to understand each other.

Now *Asal*, in his earnest desire to obtain the knowledge of things, had studied most languages and was skilful of them. So he began to speak to *Hayy Ibn Yokdhan*, and to interrogate him concerning his condition in every tongue he knew, and asked him questions concerning his doings and ways of life, and took pains to make himself understood by him. But it was all in vain: for *Hayy Ibn Yokdhan*, taking notice of all this, stood all the time wondering at what he heard, being quite at a loss to know what it all meant. He observed only the serenity of his countenance and manifest signs of goodwill. Thus they stood wrapped in wonder, looking at one another.

Asal makes Hayy eat of his food.

Now *Asal* had by him some of the remainder of the food which he had brought along with him, from the inhabited Island from whence he came. This he offered now to *Hayy Ibn Yokdhan*, but he did not know what it was; for he had never seen anything of that kind before. Then *Asal*, eating some of it himself, invited *Hayy Ibn Yokdhan* to take some of it with him. But *Hayy Ibn Yokdhan* bethought himself of those laws which he had prescribed to himself concerning the taking of his food, and seeing he knew not the nature of those things that were set before him, and whether it was lawful for him or not to partake thereof, restrained himself from eating. Whereupon *Asal* continued urging him on and kindly invited him thereunto.

Hayy Ibn Yokdhan at last joins Asal at dinner, but repents afterwards.

At last *Hayy Ibn Yokdhan*, being desirous and very anxious to get acquainted with him, and, besides, being afraid that in continuing to insist on his refusal, he might alienate his affections from him, ventured to partake of that meat and to eat thereof. But as soon as he had tasted it and found it very pleasant to his taste, he recognised that he had done amiss by breaking his contract and the resolution and promises he had made to himself concerning his diet. Thus he became greatly repentant of what he had done, and had a mind of withdrawing himself from *Asal*, and to betake himself unto his former state by endeavouring to return to his former exercise of sublime speculation.

Asal becomes Hayy's Companion and Teacher.

When he found that this intellectual vision did not immediately return to him, he thought it best to remain with *Asal* in the sensible world, until he had thoroughly satisfied himself as to his condition, so that afterwards there might remain no further inclination towards him, and then he might return to his former state and apply himself to his former contemplation without any interruption. So he joined himself to the company and fellowship of *Asal*: and when *Asal* saw that he could not speak, he was fully assured that no danger could arise to his religion by keeping company with him; and besides he had hopes that it might come to pass that he should teach him Language, Knowledge, and Religion, when he should obtain a very great reward and a nearer approach unto God.

So *Asal* began to teach him to speak, first by showing him particular things, and pronouncing their names, and by repeating them often unto him he made him to pronounce them again, which he presently did, until he had taught him all names, and so by degrees he advanced him so far that he could speak in a very short time.

Hayy enlightens Asal on his Inner Life.

Then *Asal* began to interrogate him concerning his condition, and from whence he had come into that Island. But *Hayy Ibn Yokdhan*, in his reply, told him that he knew nothing of his own origin, nor of any father or mother that he had, but only that Roe that brought him up.

Then he described to him his whole state and manner of living, from beginning to end, and what progress he had made in knowledge, until he had attained to that degree of conjunction with God.

Then *Asal* heard from him the declaration of those truths which he related, of those essences which are separated from the sensible world and which have the knowledge of the *Essence*, of that *True One*—the Almighty and Glorious—and heard him give an account of the *Essence* of that *True One*—the Almighty and Glorious—with all his attributes, and had described to him as far as it was possible for him to describe that which he had witnessed when he had reached the joys of those that are joined unto God, and the torments and griefs of those that are separated from him.

Asal then had no doubt but that all those things which were delivered in his law, concerning the commandment of that Almighty and Glorious God, his angels and books, his messengers and the last day, Paradise and Hell—all these were resemblances of what *Hayy Ibn Yokdhan* had seen. And the eyes of his heart were opened, and his mind was enlightened, when he saw that the things which he apprehended and discerned by reason, and that which he had received by tradition ("the Original and the Copy"), agreed very well together. And now the ways of mystical interpretation became easy unto him, nor was there anything difficult or remained dark of those precepts which he had received that was not now quite plain and perspicuous.

In this way his intellectual faculty grew strong and vigorous, and he began to look upon *Hayy Ibn Yokdhan* with such admiration and respect that he greatly reverenced him, and assured himself that he was *one of the Saints of God, such as were not molested with any fear upon them, and who shall not suffer through pain.* (Koran.)

Thereupon he made himself ready to wait upon him, to imitate him, and to follow his admonitions in the performance of such works as did occur unto him, in those legal things which formerly he had learned in his religion.

Asal tells Hayy of the Island from whence he had come.

Then *Hayy Ibn Yokdhan* began to enquire of him concerning his condition and his manner of living, and *Asal* gave him an account of the state of that Island from whence he had come—what kind of people inhabited it, and what sort of life they led before that religious sect which we mentioned came among them, and how it was now, since his coming thereinto.

He also gave him an account of all those things that were delivered in the law, concerning the description of the divine world, of Paradise and the fire of Hell (Gehenna), of the awakening and resurrection of mankind, of their gathering unto Judgment, of the account then to be given up, of the scales wherein the actions of men should be weighed, and the way through which they were to pass.

Now, *Hayy Ibn Yokdhan* understood very well all those things, nor did he perceive that any of them were unsuitable to that which he had seen when in that exalted condition; and he knew that he who had described those things and delivered them unto men, was true in so declaring them, and that in these his sayings he was a true and faithful messenger sent from God. And he believed him and acknowledged the truth thereof and bore testimony to his mission.

Then he began to ask him concerning the precepts which the messenger of God had delivered and the rites of worship which he had ordained. Thus *Asal* told him of *Prayer*, *Alms*, *Fasting*, and *Pilgrimage*, and the like external works: which he received and practised, and took upon him the performance thereof, in obedience to that command of the Lawgiver, being persuaded and assured of the truth and faith of him who delivered the same. Notwithstanding, there were *two things* that fixed themselves into his mind which he wondered at, neither could he perceive wherein the wisdom thereof consisted.

One of those two things was, why this messenger of God, in describing most things that relate to the divine world, used to express them unto men by parables of similitudes and abstained from a clear unfolding thereof, which caused a good many men to fall into that error by affirming corporeity in God and believing that to be something of that *Essence* the *True One*, the Almighty and Glorious, from which, however, it is absolutely free, and in the same manner concerning those things which relate to the rewards and punishments of a future world.

The other was why he did not proceed beyond those precepts and rites of worship, permitting men to seek after riches and the amassing of wealth, and to enjoy their liberty as to the matter of food: by which means they vainly delivered themselves unto vain things and turned themselves away from the truth. Whilst his judgment was that nothing ought to be taken from any; but only so much as may enable him to sustain the remainder of his life. But as to riches, he considered them of no value at all.

Now when he saw what was laid down and prescribed in the law concerning those things that belonged to the employment of riches, namely alms, and the distribution thereof and trading with them, also with regard to usury, mulcts, and punishments, these things seemed all very odd and uncouth unto him, and he judged them to be quite superfluous. For he said that if men would judge of the matter according to truth, they would certainly withdraw themselves from those vain things, and only follow the truth, so that all this would be quite superfluous, nor would any man challenge the property in riches as to have those dues exacted from him, or to cause his hands to be cut off for those things secretly stolen, or that lives should be destroyed by taking them away openly.

Hayy observes that men are dull, stupid and brutish.

This was what he thought; and that which put this opinion into his mind was that he thought that all men were imbued with an ingenuous temper, a penetrating understanding, and a mind constant unto themselves. Nor did he know how stupid and dull they were, how ill advised and how inconstant in their resolutions; so much so that they were entirely like brutes, even more apt than they to wander out of the way.

Therefore, since he was greatly affected with pity towards mankind, and anxiously desired that he might be an instrument in their salvation, a resolution entered into his mind of going over to them that he might be able to unfold and lay before them the truth of things. This desire he therefore made known to his companion *Asal*, and asked whether he could find out any way whereby he could come unto them and discourse with them.

Asal persuades Hayy to follow him to his Island.

Asal, on the other hand, told him what sort of people they were—how much lacking in ingenuousness, and how averse from obeying the commandments of God. But *Hayy* could not understand this; and his mind was intent upon that which he hoped to compass. *Asal* also greatly desired that it would please God, by his means, to direct some of his acquaintances which were of a more pliable temper and more easily to be guided than the rest, and not so far distant from sincerity as the others, into the right way. Thus he was ready to support the design of *Hayy Ibn Yokdhan.*

Hayy and Asal return together to Asal's Island.

Thereupon they resolved to betake themselves unto the seashore, nor to depart thence either by day or night till God should please to afford them an opportunity of crossing the sea. And always they were intent upon this thing, and continued with their prayers and supplications to God to direct them in this work and bring it to a successful issue.

At last it came to pass, by the commandment of God, the Almighty and Glorious, that the winds and waves drove a ship that had lost its course to the shore of that Island. And as it drew nearer unto the land, they who were in it, seeing two men upon the shore, made towards them. Then *Asal* bespeaking them, expressed the desire that they should carry them with them; they readily acquiesced therein, took them both into the ship; and it pleased God to send them a fair wind, which in a very short time conveyed them unto the desired Island. There they landed and went into the City.

Now, the friends of *Asal* all gathered round him, and he gave them an account of *Hayy Ibn Yokdhan.* Whereupon they flocked together from every side, surrounding him with reverence and admiration. Then *Asal* told him that this sect was superior in understanding and sharpness of comprehension to all others, so that if he were not able to instruct them in the truth and work upon them, there was much less hope that he would be able to teach the ordinary lot of men.

Hayy begins to teach and instruct Salaman's subjects.

Now the Sovereign and Prince of that Island was *Salaman* the friend of *Asal*, of whom we have given an account above. He was the one who thought it best to join and apply himself to human society, and considered it unlawful to give himself over to solitude. Therefore *Hayy Ibn Yokdhan* began to instruct them and to explain the mysteries of wisdom unto them. But when he began, and had proceeded a little beyond that which was plain and obvious to them, and began to inculcate that which was quite contrary to their notions deeply rooted in their minds, they began to withdraw themselves from him, and their minds abhorred from what he spoke. And inwardly in their hearts they were very angry with him, though in his presence they made a great show of kindness, both because he was a stranger and out of regard to his friend Asal.

Hayy despairs of being able to reform the vulgar crowd.

Hayy Ibn Yokdhan, however, continued day and night to deal gently with them and manifest the truth both in private and public, which only increased their hatred towards him and made them avoid his company; though otherwise they were lovers of that which is good, and desirous of the truth. But from that defect in their nature, they did not search for it in the right manner nor apprehend it as they should do: but sought the knowledge of it after the common way, like the rest of the world, after the vulgar fashion: so in the end he despaired of reforming them, and lost all hope of bringing them unto a better condition which was less acceptable unto them, because he perceived they were not willing to accept what he taught them.

Hayy's philosophical views on the value of this world.

And afterwards looking round about him and reviewing the several ranks and orders, degrees and conditions of men, he found that every sect and company of them rejoiced in those things which they had and possessed at present, and that their lusts and appetites were their God, and that they destroyed and lost themselves by gathering together the trifles and vanities of the world, the eager desire of getting them into their hands still captivating and blinding them until they tottered to their graves; and that no good counsel prevailed upon them, and that disputing with them had only the effect of making them the more obstinate. As to wisdom, they had no way open to it or access thereto, nor did any portion thereof belong unto them. "For folly has wholly overwhelmed them, and what they eagerly sought after has corrupted their hearts as rust; God has sealed up their hearts and ears, a thick mist is before their eyes, and a sore punishment awaits them." (Koran.)

Thus he saw that they were encompassed within the cauldrons of punishment and covered over with the darkness of a veil, and that all of them—a few only excepted—minded their religion no otherwise than with respect to the world, and cast the observance of religious performances behind their backs, and made little or no account thereof, and that merchandise and trading took up their minds and diverted them from thinking upon God, so that they had "no fear of that day in which both their hearts and eyes shall be turned round" (Koran)—continually employed about their worldly affairs. When he saw all this, it was apparent to him, and he held it for certain, that it was impossible for him to speak unto them to any purpose, and that it was not expedient that any works should be enjoined unto them beyond this measure, and that the greatest benefit which accrued to the common sort of men by the law was wholly in relation to their life in this world, namely, that the course and manner of their life, whilst they continued here, should proceed on in good order, so that none of them should be injurious to another in the things which he may call his own; he saw that none of them attain unto the felicity of another world but some very few, viz. those who prepare themselves to that world and rightly endeavour to attain to the same; that is, such as believe and follow the truth: but "to him that erred from the truth, and prefers the life of the present world before it, Hell shall be his place of habitation." (Koran.)

And what labour can be greater, and what misery more grievous, than his who works, if you well observe, from the time he awakes till he goes to sleep again; there will not be found so much as one amongst them who does anything but what tends to the attaining of some one or other of these vile sensible things that are of no value, to wit, either riches—to heap them up, or pleasure which he may take, or lust whereby to satisfy his mind, or wrath and revenge whereby he may satisfy his mind, or power whereby to defend himself, or some outward work commanded by the law, whereof he may make a vain-glorious show or whereby he may care to save his neck? "Now all these are darkness upon darkness in the deep sea: nor is there any of you who doth not go in thither: for such is the unchangeable decree of the Lord." (Koran.)

When, therefore, he understood the state and condition of men to be such as this, and seeing that most of them might be justly ranked amongst unreasonable creatures—were, in fact, like brute beasts—he knew that all wisdom, discretion and success was grounded on and consisted in that which the messengers of God spoke and the law delivered, and that there was no other rule possible, and that there could be nothing added to it, and that these were men appointed to every work, and every one was mostly capable of that thing unto which he was ordained by nature: and that the law of God was the same unto those that had gone away before, neither was there any change in the law of God.

Hayy gives up his Preachings and Teachings.

Whereupon, returning to *Salaman* and his companions, he craved pardon for those things that he had spoken amongst them and desired to be excused, and told them that he was of the same opinion with them, and went on in the same way and persuaded them to stick firmly to their resolution of respecting and following the customs of the law and the performance of the external rites without intruding themselves upon things that did not concern them or intermeddling therewith, that in doubtful things they should give credit and yield a ready assent to those rules that they had of old received: that they should be averse to novel opinions and to their appetites, and follow the examples of their good Forbears, and leave novelties severely alone.

He also commanded that they should shun and avoid that neglect of the laws that is seen in the vulgar sort of men, and the love of the world, and this he specially bade them to take heed of: for he and his friend *Asal* well knew that there was no salvation to this weak, tractable, and defective sort of men but by this means; and that if they were forced away and raised above this to curious speculations, their condition would be much worse, so much so that it would be impossible for them to obtain the state and degree of the Blessed; but that they would be wavering in their motives, and tossed up and down, and at last meet with a bad end. But if they remained in that state of things in which they were till death overtook them, they should obtain salvation and should be placed amongst those that are on the right hand. But, on the other side, as for those who had gone before and outwent them, those came near unto them: yet these came next after and approached near to them.

Asal and Hayy return to their Island.

Thus *Asal* and *Hayy*, after this admonitory talk, having bid farewell to Prince Salaman and his people, took leave of them and waited for an opportunity of returning to their own Island, till at length it pleased God, the Almighty and Glorious, to afford them a commodious passage thither. And *Hayy Ibn Yokdhan* endeavoured to attain to his lofty state of speculation in the same manner as formerly, until he attained thereto: and *Asal* followed his steps till he came near him or was not far therefrom. So they continued worshipping God in that Island until death seized upon them.

Epilogue of the Author.

And this is that—God help thee and us by his spirit—which we have received of the history of *Hayy Ibn Yokdhan* and *Asal* and *Salaman.*

In its setting down we have made such choice of words as are not found in any other book nor accustomed to be heard in common and vulgar speech. And it is part of that hidden knowledge which no man receives but he who has the knowledge of God; nor is any man ignorant of it, but those that have not the right knowledge of God. We have indeed followed a method quite contrary to that of our good Forbears, as to their keeping secret these matters and their sparingness of divulging them. But the reason that readily persuaded us to divulge this secret, and to break through this veil, was, these evil opinions which have risen up in this our time, the corrupt notions which are being devised by some pretenders to philosophy in this world, so that they are dispersed and diffused into various regions, and the mischief and evil arising therefrom has grown epidemical. So that we are solicitous on behalf of the weak—who have rejected what they received by tradition from the Prophets of blessed memory and make choice of that which is delivered them by foolish men—lest they should think those opinions to be a secret that ought to be kept from them who are not capable thereof, and this should increase their desire after them, and would awake a more eager appetite after them.

Therefore, it seemed good to us to give them a glimpse of this secret of secrets, whereby we may lead them into the way of truth and divert them from that wrong path.

Nevertheless, we have not committed the secrets that are comprehended in these leaves as to leave them without a thin veil which will be easily unveiled by those who are capable of understanding them, but shall be so thick and gross to those who are unworthy to go further on and pass beyond it, that it will be impossible for him to pierce through it.

And now, I crave pardon of those of my brethren as shall read this treatise, that they would excuse me with regard to those things which I have so readily declared and so freely described. For I would not have done this, unless I had been carried and elevated to such heights as transcend the reach of human sight, which cannot attain thereunto. I endeavoured to render my discourse easy to be understood, by fitly placing and ordering its parts so that I might stir up in men a keen desire to enter into the right way. But I crave of the Lord pardon and forgiveness, and that He will please to bring us to the true and certain knowledge thereof. For he is bounteous and liberal of His favours. Peace be to thee, my brother, whose promotion is decreed, and the mercy and blessing of God come upon thee.

Praise be unto God alone.

THE END.